Fact Finders™

Questions and Answers: Countries

South Korea

A Question and Answer Book

by Susan E. Haberle

Consultant:
Thomas Duvernay
Professor
Dong Guk University
Kyongju, South Korea

Capstone
press

Mankato, Minnesota

Fact Finders is published by Capstone Press,
151 Good Counsel Drive, P.O. Box 669, Mankato, Minnesota 56002.
www.capstonepress.com

Library of Congress Cataloging-in-Publication Data
Haberle, Susan E.
    South korea: a question and answer book / by Susan E. Haberle.
    p. cm.—(Fact finders. Questions and answers. Countries)
    Includes bibliographical references and index.
    ISBN 0-7368-3761-2 (hardcover)
    1. Korea (South)—Juvenile literature. 2. Korea (South) I. Title. II. Series.
DS902.12.H33 2005
951.95—dc22   2004009814

Summary: Describes the geography, history, economy, and culture of South Korea in a
    question-and-answer format.

Editorial Credits
Donald Lemke, editor; Kia Adams, set designer; Kate Opseth, book designer; Nancy Steers,
    map illustrator; Wanda Winch, photo researcher; Scott Thoms, photo editor

Photo Credits
AP/Wide World Photos/Lee Jin-man, 19; Art Directors/Trip, 12–13, 27; Corbis/Bettmann, 7;
Corbis/Catherine Karnow, 15; Corbis/Chris Lisle, cover (background); Corbis/Reuters/Kim
Kyung-Hoon, 9; Craig J. Brown, 21, 23; Folio Inc./Jeff Greenberg, 25; John Elk III, 17; Kay
Shaw Photography, 4, 20; Photo courtesy of Paul Baker, 29 (coins); Photo courtesy of Richard
Sutherland, 29 (bill); Photodisc/Neil Beer, 1; Root Resources/Mary and Lloyd McCarthy,
cover (foreground), 11; StockHaus Ltd., 29 (flag)

Artistic Effects
Photodisc/Siede Preis, 16

1 2 3 4 5 6 10 09 08 07 06 05

Table of Contents

Features

Where is South Korea?

South Korea is a small country on the Korean **Peninsula**. The peninsula sticks out from northeastern China. It is about the size of the U.S. state of Utah. The peninsula is split into two parts. North Korea covers the northern part. South Korea makes up the southern half.

Forested mountains surround many South Korean valleys. ▶

4

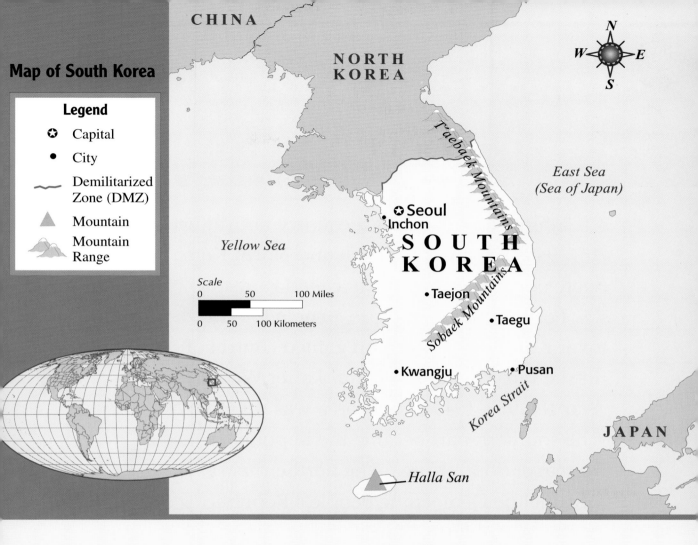

Map of South Korea

Legend

- ✪ Capital
- ● City
- ～ Demilitarized Zone (DMZ)
- ▲ Mountain
- ⛰ Mountain Range

CHINA

NORTH KOREA

Yellow Sea

East Sea (Sea of Japan)

✪ Seoul
● Inchon

SOUTH KOREA

T'aebaek Mountains

Sobaek Mountains

● Taejon

● Taegu

● Kwangju

● Pusan

Korea Strait

JAPAN

▲ — Halla San

Scale

0   50   100 Miles

0   50   100 Kilometers

Mountains cover much of South Korea. The T'aebaek Mountains stretch along the east coast. Halla San is the country's tallest peak. It is located on one of South Korea's many islands.

When did South Korea become a country?

South Korea became a country on August 15, 1948. The areas of South and North Korea were once a single country called Korea.

For thousands of years, people fought over Korea. In 1910, Japan gained control of the country. Japan lost control after World War II (1939–1945), and Korea was divided. The southern part became the Republic of Korea, or South Korea. The northern part became the Democratic People's Republic of Korea, or North Korea.

Fact!

Many people want to make North and South Korea one country again. In 2000, leaders from both countries discussed ways to reach this goal.

The first president of South Korea, Dr. Syngman Rhee (right), met with U.S. General Douglas MacArthur on August 15, 1948. They celebrated South Korea becoming a country.

The Korean War (1950–1953) started when North Korea attacked South Korea. Both sides were still angry when the fighting stopped. Since then, a wide border called the Demilitarized Zone (DMZ) has kept the countries apart.

What type of government does South Korea have?

South Korea is a democratic republic. This system of government is like the U.S. government. South Korea has three branches of government. They are the **executive branch**, the **legislative branch**, and the **judicial branch**.

Fact!

In South Korea, people must be at least 20 years old to vote in elections.

Members of the South Korean government meet at the National Assembly Hall in Seoul.

South Koreans elect a president and other leaders. The president is head of the executive branch. The president of South Korea serves one five-year term. Members of the National Assembly form the legislative branch. Voters elect the 273 members to four-year terms.

What kind of housing does South Korea have?

South Koreans live in apartments and houses. Since the 1950s, many people have moved to large cities for jobs. Most of these people live in high-rise apartments or small houses. Many homes in South Korea have computers with high-speed Internet.

Where do people in South Korea live?

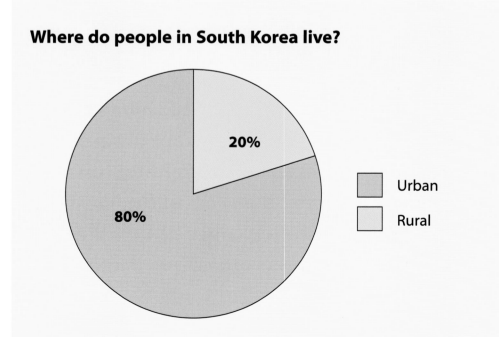

20%

80%

Urban

Rural

Some South Koreans live in traditional homes with tile roofs.

In areas outside cities, people live in small houses. These homes are made of clay, brick, or cement. Most Koreans heat their houses with underground pipes. This heat system is called *ondol* heating. Many families eat their meals while sitting on the warm floor.

What are South Korea's forms of transportation?

South Koreans use many ways to get around. In cities, people ride in buses, cars, and taxis. They also pedal bikes or walk. In large cities, people travel on subways. The capital city of Seoul has one of the largest subway systems in the world.

Most people who live outside cities travel by car or train. They drive their cars on large highways called expressways. Modern trains allow people to travel through most of the country.

Fact!

People in South Korea use ferryboats to travel to and from islands along the coast.

In cities, South Koreans travel in taxis, cars, and buses.

South Korea also has many airports. The country has its own airline called Korean Air. This airline takes people to countries around the world.

What are South Korea's major industries?

Many people in South Korea work in service and **manufacturing** jobs. People in the service **industry** work at restaurants and stores. Manufacturing workers make cars, computer parts, clothing, and other goods. South Korea ships these products to countries around the world.

What does South Korea import and export?

Imports	Exports
grains	cars
oil	clothing
steel	electronics

South Koreans buy traditional clothing at city markets.

Many South Koreans farm and fish. Farmers grow rice, wheat, peaches, and plums. They also grow an herb called ginseng. People use it in medicine and food. South Korean fishers catch shellfish and herring off the country's coasts.

What is school like in South Korea?

Children in South Korea begin six years of grade school when they are 6 years old. They then spend three years in middle school. They study many subjects, including **morals**, math, science, and Korean. Students also learn English.

Fact!

Starting in third grade, South Korean students study one to two hours of English every week.

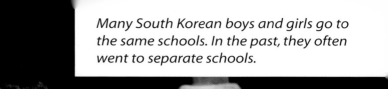

Many South Korean boys and girls go to the same schools. In the past, they often went to separate schools.

After middle school, students in South Korea go to high school. They can choose from general and vocational high schools. General schools prepare students for college. Vocational schools help train students for jobs.

What are South Korea's favorite sports and games?

Tae kwon do is a favorite South Korean sport. This form of **martial arts** began in Korea. Martial artists perform movements for exercise and self-defense. In 2000, tae kwon do became an Olympic event.

Soccer is another popular sport with children and adults. In 2002, South Korea and Japan hosted the World Cup.

Fact!

South Korea has won every Olympic gold medal in women's archery since 1984.

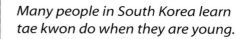
Many people in South Korea learn tae kwon do when they are young.

South Koreans also enjoy many games. One common game is *yut*. *Yut* is played with four wooden sticks and a game board. Players throw the sticks into the air. The way the sticks land shows players how many spaces to move on the game board.

What are the traditional art forms in South Korea?

Pottery is a popular art form in South Korea. Artists make vases, jars, and other objects out of clay. South Korea is known for celadon pottery. Celadon pottery is colored with a blue-green glaze.

Painting is another Korean art form. Early artists painted pictures about religion and life. They often painted on **temple** walls.

A South Korean artist makes celadon pottery out of clay. ➤

Dancers wear colorful clothing during the Korean fan dance.

South Koreans also enjoy dancing and playing music. Dancers wear bright clothing. They often carry fans, baskets, or swords. Many musicians play instruments made from wood and strings.

What major holidays do people in South Korea celebrate?

New Year's Day is a major holiday in South Korea. Families play games and eat many foods. People often dress in new clothing. Children greet grandparents and other relatives. They also visit grave sites to show their respect.

Many South Koreans celebrate Buddha's birthday in May. Buddha was the founder of a religion called **Buddhism**. People hold **rituals** at temples and have lantern parades.

What other holidays do people in South Korea celebrate?

Children's Day
Christmas Day
Constitution Day
Liberation Day

Children make paper lanterns for parades on Buddha's birthday.

The Harvest Moon Festival is another important Korean holiday. It is usually held in September or October. During this time, families celebrate the harvest of rice and other crops. The Harvest Moon Festival is like Thanksgiving Day in the United States.

What are the traditional foods of South Korea?

Two foods are basic to any Korean meal. Rice is one. The other is a pickled vegetable dish called kimchi. South Koreans have many kimchi recipes. Most recipes include a mixture of vegetables, salted sauce, red pepper, and garlic. Kimchi tastes a little like spicy sauerkraut.

Fact!

Fruit is often served for dessert in South Korea. But South Koreans serve a special rice cake on holidays. These cakes are called ddeok.

South Koreans often prepare meals with many different foods.

Most South Koreans eat with chopsticks. They cook and serve many foods in small pieces. These pieces do not need to be cut at the table.

A Korean meat dish is strips of beef soaked in soy sauce and then grilled. South Koreans call this dish *bulgogi*.

What is family life like in South Korea?

Families are important to people in South Korea. In the past, South Korean families were very large. Grandparents often lived with their children and grandchildren. Older people were highly respected.

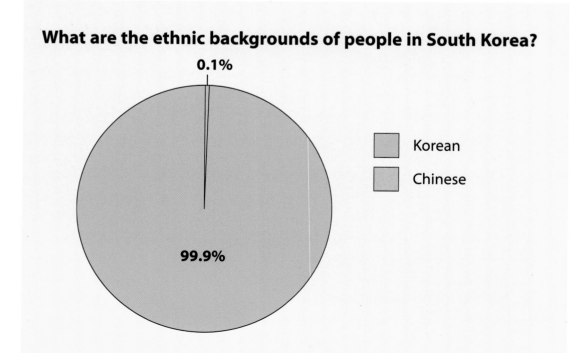

What are the ethnic backgrounds of people in South Korea?

0.1%

99.9%

- Korean
- Chinese

Many South Korean families eat meals together at low tables.

Today, many South Korean families are small. Couples usually have only one or two children. Both men and women work outside the home. Parents still teach their children respect for older people.

South Korea Fast Facts

Official name:

Republic of Korea

Population:

48,598,175 people

Land area:

*37,911 square miles
(98,189 square kilometers)*

Capital city:

Seoul

**Average annual
precipitation (Seoul):**

53 inches (135 centimeters)

Language:

Korean

**Average January
temperature (Seoul):**

*19 degrees Fahrenheit
(minus 7 degrees Celsius)*

Natural resources:

*coal, graphite, hydropower potential,
lead, molybdenum, tungsten*

**Average July
temperature (Seoul):**

*75 degrees Fahrenheit
(24 degrees Celsius)*

Religions:

Christian	*49%*
Buddhist	*47%*
Confucianist	*3%*
Other	*1%*

Money and Flag

Money:

South Korea's money is called the won. In 2004, 1 U.S. dollar equaled 1,155.5 won. One Canadian dollar equaled 882.8 won.

Flag:

South Korea's flag is called the Taegeukgi. Its white background stands for light and purity. The red and blue yin and yang symbol means harmony. The Taegeukgi has four sets of black stripes in each corner. They stand for heaven, earth, fire, and water.

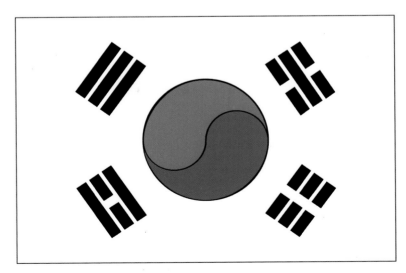

Learn to Speak Korean

Korean is the official language of the people of South Korea. Learn to speak some Korean words using the chart below.

English	Korean	Pronunciation
hello	an nyong ha seyo	(AHN YUNHG HAH say-OH)
good-bye	an nyonghi kaseyo	(AHN YUNHG-hee ka-say-OH)
please	jom	(JOHM)
thank you	kamsa hamnida	(kahm-SAH HAHM-nee-dah)
yes	yeh	(YEH)
no	aniyo	(AH-nee-yo)

Glossary

Buddhism (BOO-diz-uhm)—a religion based on the teachings of Buddha; Buddhists believe that people may live many lives in different bodies.

executive branch (eg-ZEK-yoo-tiv BRANCH)—the part of government that makes sure laws are followed

industry (IN-duh-stree)—a single branch of business or trade

judicial branch (joo-DISH-uhl BRANCH)—the part of government that explains laws

legislative branch (LEJ-iss-lay-tiv BRANCH)—the part of government that passes bills that become laws

manufacturing (man-yuh-FAK-chur-ing)—the process of making something

martial art (MAR-shuhl ART)—a style of self-defense and exercise

moral (MOR-uhl)—a belief about what is right and wrong

peninsula (puh-NIN-suh-luh)—a piece of land that is surrounded by water on three sides

ritual (RICH-oo-uhl)—a set of actions that is always performed in the same way as part of a religious ceremony or social custom

temple (TEM-puhl)—a building used for worship

Internet Sites

FactHound offers a safe, fun way to find Internet sites related to this book. All of the sites on FactHound have been researched by our staff.

Here's how:
1. Visit *www.facthound.com*
2. Type in this special code **0736837612** for age-appropriate sites. Or enter a search word related to this book for a more general search.
3. Click on the **Fetch It** button.

FactHound will fetch the best sites for you!

Read More

Feldman, Ruth Tenzer. *The Korean War.* Chronicle of America's Wars. Minneapolis: Lerner, 2004.

Italia, Bob. *South Korea.* The Countries. Edina, Minn.: Abdo, 2002.

Kwek, Karen, and Johanna Masse. *Welcome to South Korea.* Welcome to My Country. Milwaukee: Gareth Stevens, 2003.

Marquette, Scott. *Korean Conflict.* America at War. Vero Beach, Fla.: Rourke, 2003.

Index